WOMAN TO WOMAN
Reflections From the Heart

Claudette Hart

ARTHUR H. STOCKWELL LTD
Torrs Park   Ilfracombe   Devon
Established 1898
www.ahstockwell.co.uk

British Library Cataloguing-in-Publication Data.
A catalogue record for this book is available
from the British Library.

ISBN 978-0-7223-3954-1
Printed in Great Britain by
Arthur H. Stockwell Ltd
Torrs Park   Ilfracombe
Devon

DEDICATION

To my mother, Beryl, and sisters, Audrey and Diana.
Thank you for your love and prayers.

INTRODUCTION

These poems and quotes are a collection of my thoughts,
feelings and observations as I go about my daily life.
Some may make you smile, nod, laugh or cry.
My prayer is that, by reading this book, you will be drawn into
a deeper and more meaningful relationship with God.
Come journey with me.

Claudette Hart

CONTENTS

QUOTES

QUOTES

- With God all things are possible – even the impossible.

- Death puts everything into perspective.

- Lord, help us to be beautiful – the kind of beauty You delight in.

- You made preparations to go, but forgot to say goodbye.

- It's winter, but spring is coming.

- The best apparel to wear is a smile.

- Fear comes in all sorts of shapes and sizes.

- Don't let fear rob you of receiving what God has in store for you.

- It's not about the song or the singer – it's about God.

- Help us to accept from Your hand what You see fit to give.

- Where you are right now is not where you're meant to stay.

- When we feel crushed, rejected, unloved, lonely and unwanted, He gives love, joy, peace, contentment, security and acceptance.

- If God never told us why he allows or doesn't allow certain things in our lives, would we still trust him – or would we want answers first?

- Stolen water is sweet, but it leaves a bitter taste.

- Doubt, fear and unbelief can cause us to miss out on God's promises.

- Sometimes we're so preoccupied longing for the one that got away that we miss the one who's shown up.

- God can take our impossible situations and make them possible.

- Peter never knew he could walk on water until he stepped out of the boat; and we'll never know what we can do until we step out and trust God.

- God longs to do much more for us, but the devil uses fear to rob us of God's blessings.

- God has set before us an open door, but we need to walk through it.

- When the Lord lays something on your heart, do it – you never know if you will get a second chance.

- Just because God is in the boat doesn't mean we won't have any storms.

- Things change, times change, people change, situations and circumstances change – but God remains changeless.

- God's blessings do not come in half measures – He fills the cup to overflowing.

- When we play it safe we're saying we have everything under control; when we take a risk we're saying God is in control.

- God has made all the preparations; our part is to step out in faith.

- Opportunity knocks, but we have to open the door.

- Be comfortable in your own skin – you won't find a better fit!

- Don't let fear stop you from saying *yes* to God.

- Don't just believe, activate your faith.

- You are my strength, You are my song; You are my hope, my everything.

- Your words embrace me.

- Pray and let go!

- God can turn our dreams into reality.

- My child, I know you do not understand, but just continue to hold My hand and trust Me.

- God raises up different people at different times for different purposes.

- Hope refuses to lie down and admit defeat.

- As we take a step of faith the next step will be made clear.

- Blind faith is when we can't see what's over the fence or around the corner.

- If God has closed a door, start looking for the one He's about to open.

- I can't run a marathon, but I can take a step.

- Faith is stepping out into the unknown and finding Christ is already there.

- Hold on until God says, "Let go."

- Sometimes when we say *yes* to God others say *no* to us.

- Love doesn't give up at the first hurdle – it perseveres to the end.

- God's plans can never be aborted.

- Our life stories are not finished until the Author of Life writes the final chapter.

- Don't let the fragrance die with you – share it with others so that it will linger on long after you've gone.

- Every dog has its day – except for the ones who miss the boat!

- For every minus, there's a plus.

- Focus on Christ, not the crisis.

- Lord, make us content in our discontent.

- When we step out in faith, the Lord meets us on the way.

- Sometimes the hardest decisions bring the greatest blessings.

- When Christ is in the driving seat, we can go to sleep.

- One step leads to another, but it starts with that first step.

- When God gives us the answer, we don't need to get a second opinion from anyone else.

- Sometimes we get so involved in other people's calling that we miss our own.

- A little encouragement sets us on the road to success – a criticism can set us on the road to failure.

- I open my mouth to speak, but no words are forthcoming – only a deep sigh.

- Sometimes we will step on people's toes when we step out in obedience to God.

- Unless we expect it, we haven't really believed.

- Some people are so scared of making a mistake that they never make a move.

- Giving birth to our dreams can oftentimes be a long and painful process.

- It is better to walk in the dark with someone who knows the way, than to walk in the light with someone who doesn't.

- Sometimes God uses a thorn in the flesh to get us out of our comfort zone.

- Never give anyone permission to steal your joy.

- Sometimes we feel trapped inside a situation, and it's only God who can turn the key and set us free.

- Too many times we major on minor.

- If you pray for rain, make sure you take your umbrella.

- Change is here to stay.

- We need to develop an attitude of gratitude.

POEMS

WHAT IS SACRIFICE?

It is giving when you don't have.

It is letting go when you want to hold on, or holding on when you feel like letting go.

It is reaching out when you want to withdraw.

It is showing forgiveness when you want to hold a grudge.

It is smiling when you want to cry.

It is loving the unlovable, going that extra mile, and being prepared to lay down your life for others.

WHY ARE YOU CRYING?

I'm crying because of all the yesterdays I've missed and all the tomorrows I don't know about.

I'm crying because You're the only One who understands my tears.

I'm crying because I sometimes forget that You are ultimately in control.

I'm crying because I've forgotten how much You love me.

I'm crying because all my tears are stored in Your bottle.

I'm crying because one day I know You'll dry all my tears.

MY ALL IN ALL

You are my Light in the dark,
My Bread when I'm hungry,
My Living Water when I'm thirsty,
The Way when I'm lost,
My Friend when I'm lonely,
My Comforter when I'm sad,
My Teacher when I need wisdom,
My Shelter in the storm –
You are my All in All.

SUSPICIOUS

What is *suspicious*?
Is it a steady gaze or shifty eyes?
Maybe a nervous laugh or a quiet whisper?
Is it a large bag or bulging pockets?
Is it speaking in a foreign language,
Body piercing or tattoos?
Tell me: what exactly is *suspicious*?

THE CHRISTIAN WALK

The Christian walk is sometimes a tiring walk,
Sometimes a lonely walk,
Sometimes a frustrating walk;
But it is never a dull walk.

FEAR

God, deliver us from the fear of failure,
Fear of other people's opinions,
Fear of other people's disapproval,
Fear of what others will think,
Fear of what others will say,
Fear of what others will do,
Fear of trying something new.

GO FORWARD!

Go forward!
Lord, I want to obey You, but how?
Go forward!
Lord, couldn't I just go back?
Go forward!
Lord, have You seen what's ahead?
Go forward!
OK, Lord, there's no going back
So I will take a step of faith and
Go forward!

CLOSURE

Closure – final, finito, finished, the end.
The curtain has closed, time to step down and move on.
One chapter finished, a new one to begin.
New life, new plans, new hopes, new dreams;
New me; new you.

I DARE YOU!

I dare you to believe all God's promises are true!

I dare you to trust Him unfailingly!

I dare you to believe He will provide for all your needs, that He will come through for you when your back is against the wall!

I dare you to believe that He's heard your prayer and will make a way for you!

I dare you to take Him at His word and believe that all things will work for your good!

I dare you to hold on and believe when every fibre of your being screams, "This is futile – let go!"

I dare you!

I dare you!

Get thee behind me, Satan!
All God's promises are true!
He's heard my prayer and will come through for me!
He is my refuge and my fortress – my God in whom I trust!

GREY HAIR

This is a part of who I am.
It says God has brought me a mighty long way;
It says I'm comfortable in my skin;
It says I don't have a problem with it, so why should you?
It says I am liberated to be who I am;
It says I don't feel the need to conform;
It says I am grey and proud –
It says I am accepted and loved in the Beloved.

CAN'T BE BOTHERED

I just can't be bothered to be friendly,
To smile and greet you,
To make polite conversation.
Just can't be bothered to pick up the phone to call,
Or write or visit – just really can't be bothered.

Thank you, God, that You never give up on us,
Even when we give up on others
And can't be bothered to be bothered!

FAITH IN ACTION

Lord, the cupboard is bare,
The fridge is empty,
My purse is dry;

But I've prayed for You to supply my needs.
I'm trusting that You will answer,
And so in faith I'm setting the table
In preparation for the meal You will provide.

THANKING YOU

Lord, I'm thanking You right now –
I'm not going to wait until my circumstances change,
I'm thanking you right now.
Even when I can't see the light at the end of the tunnel,
I will still give thanks because the victory is in the praise.
As we take that first step of faith You will meet us halfway.
You alone are able to do far more than we could ask,
Think or imagine.

ॐ

'I being on the way, the Lord helped me.'

GENEROUS

Generous is the word that best describes you.

You are generous with your time –
You're always ready and willing
to offer help and support to others.

You are generous with your friends –
You're never selfish in keeping them to yourself.

You are generous with your home –
It is always open to welcome family, friends and visitors alike.

You are generous with your love –
You're never too busy to show love and concern to others.

Yes, *generous* is the word that best describes you!

SOMETIMES

Lord, sometimes I wish I could go somewhere
Where there is no guilt or filth; no crime or grime –
Someplace where I could bask in Your purity,
Beauty and glory.

ℬ

'I go to prepare a place for you so that where I am there you will be also.'

John 14:2

YOU SAID YOU WOULD CALL

You said you would call, and so I wait for the silence to be
broken by the ringing tone.

You said you would call, and so I listen intently for your call.

You said you would call, and so I sit up all night and wait.

You said you would call, and I try not to doubt your word,
but as days turn into weeks and weeks into months I start to
wonder;

But you said you would call, and deep down inside
I hold on to your word and want to believe you will.

AS I GET OLDER

As I get older, I want to mature like fine wine.

As I get older, I want to get wiser like an old sage.

As I get older, I want to gracefully surrender the things of youth.

As I get older, I want to put away childish things and childish ways.

As I get older, I want to become more aware that it's only Your grace and mercy that will help me, as I get older.

BEING ME

I like being me!
I like the person I am and the person I have become –

But others tell me, "That's not allowed!
You should be more accommodating, more tolerant."

I have accepted myself with all my faults, failures and
imperfections, and therefore find it easier to accept others as
they are – warts and all!

And that's the reason why I like being me!

COUNTERFEIT

Pretty, shiny, beautiful, polished and glossy –
All very attractive and appealing.

But take a closer look:
It's not genuine; it's flawed, a sham, a very good imitation –
A counterfeit.

IN TRANSIT

I'm just in transit here on earth, I'm only passing through.
The scenery may be enticing, but I'm looking forward to getting home.

Sometimes I have mishaps along the way,
but I smile as I press on, 'cause I'm only here in transit,
a stranger passing through –
Looking forward to getting home and seeing my Father's face.

So, my friends, when life's struggles get you down, just pause for a
while and remember that we're only here in transit,
This isn't our final home.
We're only foreigners and strangers, briefly passing through.

SEASONS

A time to give and a time to take,
A time to sit and a time to stand,
A time of plenty and a time of want,
A time to go and a time to stay,
A time to encourage and a time to rebuke,
A time to hold on and a time to let go,
A time to lean and a time to stand tall,
A time for hellos and a time for goodbyes,
A time to create and a time to destroy,
A time to work and a time to play,
A time to lie down and a time to rise up,
A time to trust and a time to obey.

LONGING FOR THE MORNING

Sometimes when I cannot sleep, I toss and turn and long for the morning –

But one day I will no longer be longing for the morning, when I awake in the presence of the Bright and Morning Star.

ON YOUR CASE

When you're way down in the pits and feel forgotten and forsaken,
Can you still believe that I'm on your case?

When the prison doors shut tight after you've done what you
thought was right, and you feel no one really cares,
Can you still believe that I'm on your case?

When you've given all that you have, but instead of gratitude all
you get is criticism,
Can you still believe that I'm on your case?

When your back is up against the wall, and you have no one to turn to,
Can you really still believe that I will *always* be on your case?

ACCEPTANCE

Do you accept me because of my long, flowing hair?
My lovely manicured nails? My long, dark lashes?
My shining white teeth, or my bright, sparkling eyes?
Maybe it's my plump breasts, or my flat tummy?

The reality is my hair is synthetic, my nails are acrylic, my lashes
are Maybelline, my teeth are chemically whitened, my eyes are
contact lenses, my breasts are silicone and my tummy is lipo'ed –
Oh, and my hair colour is from a bottle and my tan is from a salon.

So, now you know all about me, do you still accept me?

BROWN-PAPER PACKAGE

A thing of value can often be disguised in brown-paper packaging.

We need to invest time and effort to unwrap the outer layer to see what's hidden inside.

Sometimes we miss the good qualities in others because they come wrapped in a brown-paper packaging, while we look for the gold-and-silver package tied up with pretty pink bows.

CAN YOU STILL BELIEVE?

Can you still believe when all around you is falling apart?

Can you still believe when you see your dreams come crashing down?

Can you still believe when there's no light at the end of the tunnel?

Can you still believe when you have nothing left to cling to?

Can you still believe when you feel God has forsaken you?

Yes, Lord, even as I go through the lowest point of my life,
I still choose to believe.

'BUT GOD . . .'

When you've tried and failed and feel like giving up,
Remember, 'But God . . .'

When you feel deserted, abandoned and forsaken,
Remember, 'But God . . .'

When the devil tells you you've messed up and God can't use
you, Remember, 'But God . . .'

'But God . . .' Two words that can stem the tide and turn things
around.

'But God . . .' With Him all things are possible.

'But God . . .' He has not given up on you, so don't give up on
Him.

'But God . . .' reminds me that He is not through with me yet, so
when I feel like giving up I will hold on tight and say,
"But God . . ."

SEIZE THE MOMENT!

Some people would say, "Seize the day," but oftentimes we
don't have a day, only a brief moment in time.

So take full advantage of that moment, however brief it may be,
and make the most of the opportunity, because for some, that's all
the time they will have.

BUMP IN THE ROAD

What do you do when you come to a bump in the road?
Complain of the hassles and the jerks,
Or slow down and take it easy?

As we travel on the road of life, we will also encounter bumps,
but the way we deal with them will make the difference to how
smooth or rough a ride it will be.

The choice is ours.

LORD,

Take my failures, my fears, my weaknesses, my insecurities, my
discouragements, and replace them with Your ability, Your courage,
Your strength, Your power and everything else I stand
in need of; and help me to be all that You created me to be.

Amen.

NEW DAY

Thank You, God, for the gift of a new day –
A fresh start, a new page, a clean slate.
Help me as I go through it, that whatever is written on it
Will praise and glorify You.

Amen.

TRAVELLING COMPANIONS

Don't invite Fear to be one of your travelling companions as
you journey through life.

He will trip you up, slow you down and cripple you.
Instead of advancing, you will find yourself retreating as he
shares all the obstacles and problems you're likely to encounter.
Tell him to find his own companions: Doubt and Unbelief.

Instead, seek out Faith, Hope and Courage to journey with you.
They will encourage you, lighten your steps and enable you to
fight and win many battles on your journey of a lifetime.

THE COMPLIMENT

My feet have wings, my face is aglow, my spirit is light and
I'm on cloud nine, all because a compliment was paid.

My spirit is heavy, my face downcast and my feet drags,
all because a criticism was made.

I will therefore choose to forget the criticism, revel in the
compliment, and make the most of my day!

TITLES

I am a wife!
I am a mother!
I am a wife *and* a mother!

Me? No, I'm not a wife or a mother – I'm just *me*.

WALKING BY FAITH

Walking by faith means not knowing where the next step will lead or what's around the corner.

Walking by faith is a challenge.

Walking by faith is stepping out into the unknown, but holding tightly to God's hand.

Walking by faith is wondering where this adventure will lead.

Walking by faith is both scary and exciting.

Walking by faith is a decision of the heart.

Walking by faith is trusting a God who has our best interest at heart.

Walking by faith is knowing that when the road gets rough, He is still there and will never let us fall.

Walking by faith is letting go and letting God act on our behalf.

Walking by faith is pleasing to God.

Walking by faith is a sure sign of maturity.

Walking by faith is handing everything over to God.

Walking by faith is the only way to experience God's best for us.

Walking by faith is walking with God.

GOD BLESS MOTHERS!

God bless mothers, young and old –
New mothers and experienced mothers,
Mothers whose arms are now empty through loss of a child or
through family break-up,
Mothers whose children have flown the nest and have never
looked back,
Mothers who are proud of their children, and mothers whose
hearts are broken because of their children.
God bless mothers-to-be as they wait expectantly for their new
arrival, and God bless women who yearn to be mothers –
Those who dream of one day being proud mothers and those
whose dream will never materialise.
And, God, remember mothers who have taken on the role of
caring for other people's children as their own. Remember
single mothers who have to be both mother and father.
And, God, remember fathers who for various reasons have to
take on the role of mother and father to their children.

Yes, God bless mothers, near and far, and remember those
women who will never bear the title *Mother*.

SPENT

Sometimes we feel all spent and used up –
That we can't be of much use to God or anyone else.

But if God could breathe life into old dried-up bones, what
does that say about what He can do with your life?

HOW ARE YOU?

How am I?
Well, actually I haven't been feeling so good lately. I've been going through a rough patch and things are not as good as they could be.

I'm feeling kind of low right now and just need someone to talk to – someone who will listen and try to understand my situation.

I feel under pressure, and I'm not sure which way to turn. There's so much I want to share with somebody – anybody – and I'm so glad you asked.

But, as I turned to give an answer, I caught only a glimpse of you, as you hurriedly rushed away, with the question left hanging, unanswered, in the air.

SUDDENLY

You came into my life,
Softly, sweetly and unexpectedly,
And before I knew it you were gone,
Just as suddenly as you came –
Softly, sweetly, unexpectedly.

DILEMMA

What to do?
Should I speak up or keep quiet?
Should I hold on or let go?
Should I stand still and stagnate,
Or step forward and take a risk?

Questions, questions, questions!
Lord, You who are the Author and Finisher of my faith,
Guide me in the way I should go.

MEMORY

I invade your thoughts without invitation;
I intrude on your waking moments and leave you with
sleepless nights.

Who am I?
Your memory!

WHEN I'M GONE

'You will be missed!'
'You will be *greatly* missed!'

'When did they leave?'

PERFECT PEACE

I'm thankful to God for friends and family,
Fun and laughter,
Noise and excitement . . .

But sometimes it's good just to have peace, perfect peace.

DRY BONES

Dry bones, dry bones, can you live?
Are you just dry or are you dead?
Only You know, Lord – only You.

My spirit's dried up, my emotions have dried up,
My body's dried up.
Am I just dry, or am I dead?
Only You know, Lord – only You.

Your Spirit, which is life, breathes upon me and I live.
My spirit's alive! My emotions are alive! My body's alive!
Only You could do it, Lord – only You!

GUILTY AS CHARGED

Am I being selfish when I express my desire to love and be loved?
In wanting to experience all the range of emotions that
come as I strive to pursue my dreams, goals and expectations?

Am I being selfish in wanting your love all to myself and not
wanting to share?

If that is being selfish,
Then I'm guilty as charged!

YOU SAY . . . ; GOD SAYS . . .

"I feel lonely." *I will never leave you or forsake you.*

"I feel invisible." *I have you engraved in the palm of my hand.*

"I feel unloved." *I have loved you with an everlasting love.*

"I feel like a loser." *With me all things are possible.*

"I feel trapped." *I came to set you free.*

"I feel frustrated." *Cast your cares upon me.*

"I feel tired." *Come, and I will give you rest.*

"I feel no one cares." *I care!*

"I feel ashamed." I *don't condemn you; go and sin no more.*

"I feel hurt." *I am the Balm in Gilead.*

"I feel like a nobody." *He who touches you touches the apple of my eye.*

"I feel friendless." *I am a friend who sticks closer than a brother.*

"I feel . . . I feel . . . I feel . . ." *Hush, my child, I understand. Just trust and rest in me; and, when you come to the end of yourself, you'll find I'm all you need.*

GOD'S WAITING ROOM

Being in God's waiting room is never easy.
At first you're quite contented to sit and wait your turn,
But as time passes you start to get anxious.
Others who have come after you have been called,
While you're still waiting.

'Maybe they've forgotten I'm here.
Maybe I need to find out why it's taking so long.'

Just when you're at the point of giving up,
You hear a name being called.

Could it be? It sounded like – Yes, that's me!
My name has finally been called!
I rise and eagerly step forward as I see my Father approaching.
He greets me with a smile.

*My child, why were you so anxious? Was it because you
thought I had forgotten you? As a matter of fact, you were
never out of my mind for one second. All this waiting was
for your benefit, and what I was preparing for you could
not be rushed. The waiting that you've endured has served
to mature you to a level that could not have been achieved
otherwise. Now you are fully equipped to enjoy all the good
things I have in store for you.*

MAKING YOU SMILE

What can I do to make you smile?
You seem so sad, so preoccupied.
Maybe if I could catch your eye,
You would see that someone cares.

Take heart and do not be discouraged.
Maybe one day you will meet someone who will be able to do
something I couldn't do – make you smile.

ROUTINE, ROUTINE, ROUTINE

I'm tired of the daily routine, Lord:
Cleaning, shopping, cooking, washing,
Day in, day out.
But, on reflection, where would we be without routine?

୫

*'While the earth remains, seedtime and harvest, and cold
and heat, and summer and winter, and day and night shall
not cease.'*
Genesis 8:22

WINNING SMILE

He had such a winning smile, I found it hard to take my eyes from
his face. But, unexpectedly, my eyes were drawn to his hand, and I
realised something was wrong – it was deformed.

But still my eyes refused to stay there
and was drawn back to his face – his smile.

Lord, my prayer is that his personality, his charm, his smile, will
shine through, so that others will be drawn to him and see his
character and not his disability.
Bless him real good, Lord, and grant grace and favour to those
who love him and care for him.

APPROVAL

Why should it matter to me whether you give your approval or not?
Whether I get an approving smile, a pat on the back
or a personal endorsement?

It shouldn't really matter, and I shouldn't really care, but
deep down inside we all look for and strive to gain the
approval of others, whether they be parents, friends, teachers,
managers or spouses.

But ultimately the only thing that will truly matter is
hearing from Your lips,
"Well done, good and faithful servant."

UNDER THE MICROSCOPE

Don't put me under the microscope –
You may be disappointed by what you see.
My flaws are all too obvious to me,
And they will only be magnified by you.
Instead, take me as you see me and accept me for who I am –
Just one of the crowd.

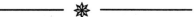

THE LAST GOODBYE

The last goodbye is the hardest goodbye of all.
It speaks of finality, termination and conclusion –
The end of a friendship, a relationship, a partnership.
Yes, when all is said and done,
The last goodbye is the hardest goodbye of all.

UNLIKELY FRIENDSHIP

Theirs was an unlikely friendship.

There was nothing obvious for others to see what drew him to her or her to him – it was an unlikely friendship.

Nevertheless, they were bound together with an invisible cord of friendship that united them as kindred spirits.

Others look on and wonder what the attraction could be, but they are content just to enjoy their very unlikely friendship.

PASSING GLANCE

It was just a passing glance, but it spoke volumes.
It spoke of possibilities, of prospects, of realization of dreams,
Of expectation and anticipation,
Of 'What if?', 'Maybe' and 'If only'.
It was only a passing glance, but it spoke volumes . . .

GRATEFUL

Lord, we come to You in our brokenness, imperfections, sin and nakedness; and You come alongside us and wrap Your arms of love, mercy, grace and forgiveness around us; and You mend us, wash us and clothe us in garments of righteousness; and we are forever grateful.